A New True Book

THE CHEYENNE

By Dennis B. Fradin

CHILDREN'S PRESS
A Division of Grolier Publishing
Sherman Turnpike
Danbury, Connecticut 06816

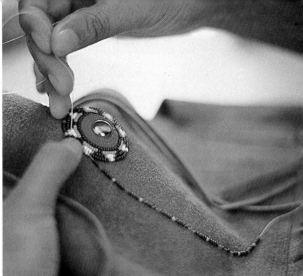

Cheyenne beadwork

For their help, the author thanks:
Floyd Black Bear, Treasurer, Cheyenne-
Arapaho tribes of Oklahoma
Tom Burns, Education Coordinator, Cheyenne-
Arapaho tribes of Oklahoma
Archie Hoffman (Flying Hawk), Cheyenne-
Arapaho tribes of Oklahoma
Diana McLean, Lame Deer, Montana
Joanne Sooktis, Lame Deer, Montana

Library of Congress Cataloging-in-Publication Data

Fradin, Dennis B.
  The Cheyenne / by Dennis B. Fradin.
      p.   cm. — (A New true book)
  Includes index.
  Summary: A brief history of the Cheyenne Indians,
who call themselves "The People."
  ISBN 0-516-01211-8
  1. Cheyenne Indians—Juvenile
literature. [1. Cheyenne Indians. 2. Indians of
North America.] I. Title.
E99.C53F73   1988   87-33792
                                      CIP
                                      AC

FIFTH PRINTING 1992
Childrens Press®, Chicago

PHOTO CREDITS

Amon Carter Museum—11

© Reinhard Brucker—15, 18, 19 (4 photos),
21 (2 photos), 28

© Joyce Langemo Camper—40

© Michael S. Crummett—2 (left), 7 (3 photos),
8 (left), 22, 24 (right), 41 (2 photos), 43 (left),
45 (left)

© Dr. Hauxwell—Cover, 4 (top), 13 (right), 26
(2 photos), 45 (right)

Library of Congress—12, 33, 34

© Jay Littlewolf—2 (right), 4 (bottom), 8 (right),
43 (right)

Museum of the American Indian—36 (left)

NorthWind Picture Archives—38

Stanley J. Morrow Collection, W.H. Over
Museum, Vermillion, SD—13 (left)

© James Rowan—24 (left), 36 (right)

Smithsonian Institution: National
Anthropological Archives—16;
National Museum of American Art—30

Maps—Al Magnus, 10

Cover: Young boy in traditional headdress

TABLE OF CONTENTS

"The People"...5

Early Cheyenne History...8

Horses Change the Cheyenne
 Way of Life...10

The Daily Life of Adults...14

Cheyenne Children...18

Cheyenne Beliefs...22

The Cheyenne at War...27

The White People Take Cheyenne
 Lands...32

The Cheyenne Today...39

Words You Should Know...46

Index...47

The traditions
of the Cheyenne
are passed from
one generation
to the next.

"THE PEOPLE"

The Cheyenne have
lived in the central and
western United States
for hundreds of years.
Until the late 1800s
the Cheyenne moved
freely about the country.
Then, after fighting many
battles against United
States soldiers, the
Cheyenne were pushed
onto reservations in
Oklahoma and Montana.

Many Cheyenne live in Oklahoma and Montana. However, the Cheyenne also live in cities across the United States. Many places are named after the Cheyenne. The Sheyenne River in North Dakota and the Cheyenne River in South Dakota and the towns of Sheyenne, North Dakota and Cheyenne, Oklahoma were named for the tribe. Cheyenne, Wyoming, the capital of the state, is also named for "The People."

Long ago, the Cheyenne began to call themselves *Tsistsistas*, meaning "The People." The Sioux Indians called them the *Shahiyena*, meaning "People of Strange

6

The Cheyenne work in many jobs, from security guards (above left) to firefighters (above). But they keep their traditions alive. Allan Rowland (left) is a former Tribal Chairman of the Northern Cheyenne.

Speech." The name *Shahiyena* was slowly changed to *Cheyenne*—the name by which the tribe is generally known today.

The early Cheyenne left rock carvings called petroglyphs.

EARLY CHEYENNE HISTORY

Very long ago the
Cheyenne are thought to
have lived in what is now
the eastern United States.

First they may have lived somewhere near Lake Superior. Then in the late 1600s they are thought to have moved to Minnesota, and after that, to the Dakotas.

In their early years, the Cheyenne lived in villages. They built earth lodges— homes made of logs, dirt, and grass. The early Cheyenne hunted, fished, and farmed. Their main crops were corn, beans, and squash.

HORSES CHANGE THE CHEYENNE WAY OF LIFE

The Great Plains

Spanish people brought the first horses to America in the 1500s. The horses bred until thousands of them were roaming in what is now the central and western United States. Native Americans caught some of these horses. The

The Medicine Man, C. M. Russell, 1908. Courtesy Amon Carter Museum, Fort Worth

Cheyenne began riding horses in about 1750.

Back then the Great Plains was home to millions of buffalo. Cheyenne hunters found it easier to kill buffalo on

Buffalo roamed the western plains.

horseback than on foot.
The buffalo provided their
people with food, clothes,
and other items.

During the late 1700s
the Cheyenne stopped
farming and abandoned
their villages. They began

following the buffalo herds
across the Great Plains.
Instead of earth lodges,
the Cheyenne began living
in tipis. Made of poles
and buffalo skins, the
tipis could be quickly
set up and taken apart.

Indian women (left) cured buffalo
skins and used them for robes and
tipi covers. Some modern campers use
tipis with canvas covers (right).

THE DAILY LIFE OF ADULTS

The Cheyenne were divided into ten large bands. The people of each band traveled about the countryside with their horses.

A typical band had several hundred people, who lived in dozens of tipis. When a man and woman married, they usually went to live near the woman's mother. The

newlyweds' tipi and its
furnishings were supplied
by their relatives.

Men and women
did different types of work.
The men did the hunting.
Among the animals they
killed were buffalo,
antelope, wild sheep, deer,
and elk. The men usually

A buffalo bull

This photo, taken on July 4, 1895, shows meat drying on a rack.

hunted buffalo in a group. They surrounded a herd, then killed some of the buffalo with their lances or bows and arrows.

The men also fished with willow nets, made weapons, and served as

the chiefs of each band.
When the Cheyenne were
at war, the men went
out to fight.

The women did most of
the child raising. They
made clothes out of the
skins of buffalo, deer, wild
sheep, and antelopes.
Women also were in
charge of the cooking and
the pottery making. They
gathered the berries, roots,
and seeds, which were used
as foods and medicines.

CHEYENNE CHILDREN

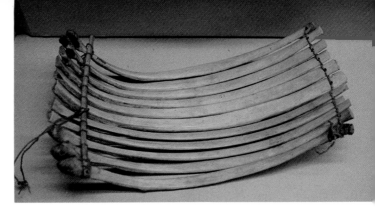

Cheyenne sled made of buffalo ribs.

Cheyenne children were taught by their relatives. By age six, Cheyenne children could ride horses bareback. By then, boys were helping their fathers herd horses and learning to do other work. Girls were helping their mothers.

Cheyenne children loved to play. Girls played

DOUBLE BALL
CHEYENNE

The leather ball (above left), doll (above), bowl and dice set, and the double ball (left) were Cheyenne playthings.

with deerskin dolls, while boys had little bows and arrows. The children also played games in which they pretended to be such animals as coyotes and bears. The children also liked to set up "play camps."

The children used little
tipis made by their
mothers. They had their
dogs drag the materials
for the tipis a short way
from home. When they found
a good place, the children
set up their play camp. They
pretended that they were
the parents, that their dogs
were the horses, and that
their baby brothers and
sisters were the children.

Boys at play camp
sometimes caught fish in

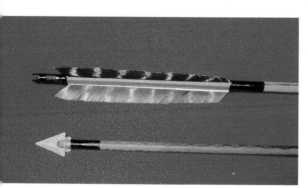

Cheyenne arrows (left) and buffalo rib knife (right)

a stream and killed birds and rabbits. The girls prepared the food. In this way the children practiced doing adult work.

By about age twelve, boys were going on buffalo hunts and learning about warfare from their fathers and uncles. Girls worked with their mothers until they were married.

Medicine
Deer Rock

CHEYENNE BELIEFS

Religion was important
in all parts of Cheyenne
life. The main spirit was
the creator, Heammawihio,
"The Wise One Above."
Heammawihio was thought
to have lived on earth

22

long ago. It was believed that he had shown the Cheyenne how to plant corn, hunt with bows and arrows, and make fire.

After living on earth for a time, Heammawihio had gone to live in the sky. The Cheyenne believed that, after death, they would join Heammawihio in heaven. They thought the Milky Way was a "Hanging Road" that the souls of the dead followed up to heaven.

Bear Butte (left) is a sacred mountain to the Sioux and Cheyenne. The bald eagle (right) is a sacred bird.

Another major spirit, Ahktunowihio, "The Wise One Below," was said to live underground. The Cheyenne believed that spirits existed in the four directions—north, south, east, and west. They also believed that certain animals had sacred powers. One of them, the Thunder Being, was said to bring the summer rains.

The Cheyenne feared underwater spirits, some of which they believed were like huge lizards. And they were afraid of ghosts, which were said to make strange noises at night.

The Cheyenne held a number of ceremonies to pray for guidance and to thank the spirits for good things they had received.

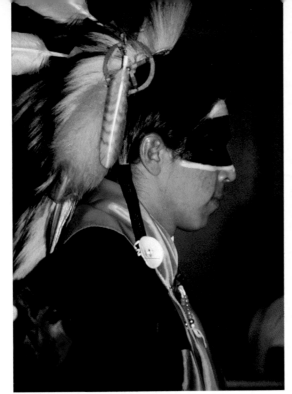

Special costumes are a vital part of tribal ceremonies.

Priests were in charge of these ceremonies, which included dances, music, and tobacco offerings. Sometimes all ten bands of the Cheyenne gathered for religious festivals.

THE CHEYENNE AT WAR

Once they began hunting buffalo on horseback, the Cheyenne sometimes entered other people's hunting grounds. Other people also sometimes entered Cheyenne hunting grounds. The result was that the Cheyenne were often at war. Among their main enemies were the Kiowa, the Crow, and the Pawnee.

This hide painting records a Cheyenne fighting man's success in battle

The Cheyenne fought on horseback with bows and arrows. Cheyenne fighters were very skilled with these weapons. Some of

them could hit moving
targets at distances of
more than a hundred yards.
The Cheyenne killed
some of their enemies.
But the bravest thing a
Cheyenne fighting man
could do was just to touch
an enemy. A man would
ride up to a foe and touch
him with a stick or other
object. Then he would
quickly ride away. This
was called "counting coup."

Wolf on the Hill, Chief of the Tribe, was painted by George Catlin in 1832. Catlin was impressed by this chief, who stood over six feet tall, as did most Cheyenne men.

Usually, each Cheyenne band fought its own wars. Sometimes, though, all ten bands joined to fight an enemy. When this happened, the Cheyenne took sacred objects belonging to the whole tribe into battle. One object was the Sacred Buffalo Hat, which was made of buffalo skin.

The four Sacred Arrows also were brought into battle. The Cheyenne believed that these objects had the power to help them win battles.

THE WHITE PEOPLE TAKE CHEYENNE LANDS

During the early 1800s, the Cheyenne divided into two main groups. The Northern Cheyenne settled in the northern part of the Great Plains of the United States. The Southern Cheyenne settled in the southern Great Plains.

During the mid-1800s, the Cheyenne began having trouble with white

Workers lay track for the Northern Pacific Railroad.

Americans. The white settlers entered Cheyenne lands for several reasons. Many came to farm, ranch, or look for gold. Others came to build railroads and trails through Cheyenne hunting grounds.

Indians pass Fort Union, Montana, on the Missouri River. The tribes were constantly pushed west by "land-hungry" settlers.

Still others came to hunt buffalo.

Like other Native Americans, the Cheyenne suffered because the settlers took over their lands. The buffalo hunters killed off their main food source.

The United States

government decided that
white Americans should
have most of the
Cheyenne hunting grounds.
During the 1860s and
1870s, the Cheyenne
fought many big battles
against U.S. soldiers. In
1876, about two thousand
Sioux and Cheyenne
joined together to fight
U.S. troops led by
George Armstrong Custer.
The battle took place at
the Little Big Horn River
in Montana. In this battle

Deerskin painting (left) is an Indian's record of the 1876 battle at the Little Big Horn. At right is an artist's idea of Custer at the battle.

the Indians killed Custer and over two hundred of his soldiers.

In the end, though, the Cheyenne could not beat the United States. The U.S. government had a bigger

army and better weapons
than the Cheyenne. Also,
the soldiers sometimes
attacked peaceful camps,
killing nearly every man,
woman, and child they
found. In one bloody
massacre, white soldiers
of the Colorado militia
killed nearly three hundred
friendly Cheyenne led by
Chief Black Kettle at Sand
Creek, Colorado.

By the 1880s the Cheyenne
had been pushed onto two
reservations. The Southern

Cheyenne were forced to move to reservations.

Cheyenne were settled in Oklahoma. The Northern Cheyenne were sent to Montana. The Indians on the reservations suffered terribly from disease, poverty, and a lack of jobs.

THE CHEYENNE TODAY

About fifteen thousand Cheyenne live in the United States today. They are still divided into the Northern Cheyenne and Southern Cheyenne.

Several thousand Northern Cheyenne live on the Northern Cheyenne Reservation around Lame Deer, Montana. Several thousand Southern

Lame Deer, Montana

Cheyenne live in
Oklahoma, where there
is no longer a Cheyenne
reservation.

Thousands of other
Cheyenne live and work in
cities and towns across
the United States.

Robert Lone Bear, a firefighter, and Gail Small, a tribal attorney, reflect the modern Cheyenne.

Although the Cheyenne live like other Americans in many ways, they have kept their special identity. In fact, few Indian tribes have maintained their traditions as well as the

Cheyenne, who still call themselves *Tsistsistas*— "The People."

Cheyenne children are given two names—an Indian name and an English name. In public, the people usually use their English names. But within their family circles, many are called by their Cheyenne names.

In addition to English many Cheyenne speak the Cheyenne language. At several schools in

Alice Kinzel (left), age 96, is the oldest member of the Northern Cheyenne. She has more than 400 descendants.

Montana, the children study both Cheyenne and English. Other Cheyenne children learn their native language from their parents or grandparents.

The elders also teach the traditional dances, songs, and stories to the young.

Some of the old religious beliefs and customs are still very much alive too. For example, the Sacred Buffalo Hat is kept by the Cheyenne in Montana, while the Sacred Arrows are held by the Cheyenne in Oklahoma. Each year, Cheyenne from around the country gather in Oklahoma for a Sacred

Arrows ceremony. There
are also other times when
Cheyenne gather in
Oklahoma or Montana for
special events. Their
strong tribal traditions
strengthen their daily lives.

45

WORDS YOU SHOULD KNOW

Ahktunowihio (ahk • toon • oh • wih • HY • oh) — "The Wise One Below," an important Cheyenne spirit

band (BAND) — a group of families that travel together; part of a larger group called a tribe

Cheyenne (SHY • an) — an Indian tribe whose members live in Oklahoma and Montana; many others are scattered across the United States

chiefs (CHEEFS) — leaders of Native American tribes

"counting coup" (KOWN • ting KOO) — touching an enemy with a stick or other object

earth lodges (ERTH • LAH • jiz) — houses made of logs, dirt, and grass

Great Plains (GRAYT PLAYNZ) — a huge, rather flat region extending from Texas up past the Dakotas and into Canada

Heammawihio (hay • ahm • mah • wih • HY • oh) — "The Wise One Above," the main Cheyenne spirit.

lance (LANS) — a weapon consisting of a long stick with a stone or metal blade at one end; a spear

massacre (MAS • ih • ker) — the killing of people who have little or no defense

militia (muh • LISH • uh) — a group of citizens who are not members of the regular army, called up to fight in emergencies

Northern Cheyenne (NOR • thern SHY • an) — a branch of the Cheyenne that stayed in the northern part of the Great Plains in the early 1800s

reservations (rez • uhr • VAY • shunz) — areas set aside by the government for Native Americans

Sacred Arrows (SAY • krid AR • ohz) — four special arrows that were believed to have the power to help the Cheyenne win battles

Sacred Buffalo Hat (SAY • krid BUFF • uh • loh HAT) — a hat made of buffalo skin that was believed to have the power to help the Cheyenne in battle

Southern Cheyenne(SUTH • ern SHY • an) —a branch of the
Cheyenne that moved to the southern Great
Plains in the early 1800s
tipis(TEE • peez) —tents made of poles covered with animal skins
Thunder Being(THUN • duhr BEE • ing) —a great bird spirit
believed to bring summer rains
Tsistsistas(sis • SIS • tahs) —"The People," the name the Cheyenne
call themselves

INDEX

Ahktunowihio, 24
antelope, 15, 17
Arrows, Sacred, 31, 44
arrows, bows and, 16, 19, 28
bands, 14, 26, 30
bareback riding, 18
battle, sacred objects in, 31
battles, 35, 36
beans, 9
bears, 19
beliefs, 22-26, 31, 44
Black Kettle, Chief, 37
bows and arrows, 16, 19, 28
boys, 18, 19, 20, 21
buffalo, 11-13, 15, 17, 21, 34
Buffalo Hat, Sacred, 31, 44
camps, children's play, 20
ceremonies, 25-26, 45
Cheyenne language, 43
Cheyenne names, 42
Chief Black Kettle, 37

children, 18-21, 42
clothes, 17
Colorado, 37
Colorado militia, 37
cooking, 17
corn, 9
"counting coup," 29
coyotes, 19
crops, main, 9
Crow people, 27
Custer, George Armstrong, 35-36
daily life, 14-17
Dakotas, the, 9
dances, 26, 44
deer, 15, 17
disease, on reservations, 38
dogs, 20
earth lodges, 9, 13
elk, 15
enemies, 27, 29, 30
English names, 42

farming, 9, 12, 33
festivals, 26
fishing, 9, 16, 20
food, 17, 34
games, children's, 19-20
girls, 18, 19, 21
Great Plains, 11, 13, 32
"Hanging Road," 23
Hat, Sacred Buffalo, 31, 44
Heammawihio, creator, 22-23
heaven, 23
herding, 18
history, early, 8-9
horses, 10-12, 18, 27, 28
hunters, 11, 34
hunting, 9, 15, 16, 20, 27, 34
hunting grounds, 27, 33, 35
Indian names, 42
Kiowa people, 27
Lake Superior, 9

Lame Deer, Montana, **39**
lands, tribal, **34**
language, **42-43**
lodges, earth, **9, 13**
massacre, **37**
medicines, **17**
men, work of, **15-17**
Milky Way, **23**
Minnesota, **9**
Montana, **5, 35, 38, 44, 45**
music, **26**
nets, willow, **16**
newlyweds, **14-15**
North Dakota, **9**
Northern Cheyenne, **32, 38, 39**
offerings, tobacco, **26**
Oklahoma, **5, 38, 40, 44-45**
Pawnee, **27**
"The People," **6-7, 42**
"People of Strange Speech," **6, 7**
"play camps," **20**
population, Cheyenne, **39-40**
pottery making, **17**
poverty, **38**
railroads, **33**
rains, **25**
ranching, **33**
religion, **26, 44**
reservations, **37-38, 39, 40**
Sacred Arrows, **31, 44, 45**

Sacred Buffalo Hat, **31, 44**
sacred objects, **31**
Sand Creek, Colorado, **37**
schools, **42-43**
Shahiyena, ("People of Strange Speech"), **6, 7**
sheep, wild, **15, 17**
Sioux people, **6, 35**
soldiers, U.S., **35-37**
songs, **44**
South Dakota, **9**
Southern Cheyenne, **32, 39, 40**
Spanish people, **10**
spirits, belief in, **22, 24, 25**
squash, **9**
Superior, Lake, **9**
Thunder Being, **25**
tipis, **13, 14, 20**
tobacco offerings, **26**
traditions, **41, 45**
tribes, **27, 41**
Tsistsistas, ("The People"), **6, 42**
United States, **34-36, 39**
villages, **9, 12**
war, **17, 27, 28, 30**
warfare, learning about, **21**
weapons, **16, 28, 37**
white people, **32-38**
"Wise One Above, The," **22**
"Wise One Below, The," **24**
women, work of, **17**

About the Author

Dennis Fradin attended Northwestern University on a partial creative scholarship and was graduated in 1967. His previous books include the Young People's Stories of Our States series for Childrens Press, and Bad Luck Tony for Prentice-Hall. In the New True Book series, Dennis has written about astronomy, farming, comets, archaeology, movies, space colonies, the space lab, explorers, the thirteen colonies, and pioneers. He is married and the father of three children.